DOTTRINA DEL FASCISMO

BENITO MUSSOLINI

Copyright © 2018 All rights reserved.
Quest'opera è tutelata dalla Legge sul diritto d'autore.
Ogni riproduzione, anche parziale, è reato perseguito.

INDICE

PREFAZIONE DEL REDATTORE 5
IDEE FONDAMENTALI 6
I 7
II 8
III 9
IV 10
V 11
VI 12
VII 13
VIII 14
IX 15
X 16
XI 17
XII 18
XIII 19
DOTTRINA POLITICA E SOCIALE 20
I 21
II 23
III 25
IV 26
V 27
VI 29
VII 31
VIII 32
IX 34
X 36
XI 38
XII 40
XIII 41

PREFAZIONE DEL REDATTORE

La prima parte dell'opera, le idee fondamentali del Fascismo, fu scritta per mano del filosofo Giovanni Gentile, già ministro dell'istruzione nel governo Mussolini (sua fu l'omonima riforma dell'istruzione scolastica, resa obbligatoria fino a 14 anni d'età) e iscritto al Partito Nazionale Fascista. Il linguaggio è quello di un letterato, e analizza in maniera profonda il Fascismo, esprimendo l'idea nei suoi principi fondamentali.

La seconda parte dell'opera, la dottrina politica e sociale, scritta di pugno da Benito Mussolini, ha un linguaggio più diretto che mette continuamente a confronto società, nazioni, idee e sistemi politici ed economici dei secoli precedenti e del XX secolo con il nascente Fascismo; spiega un nuovo concetto di Stato-Individuo e la responsabilità di questo nell'evoluzione e nella elevazione dell'uomo.

Buona lettura.

IDEE FONDAMENTALI

I

Come ogni salda concezione politica, il fascismo è prassi ed è pensiero, azione a cui è immanente una dottrina, e dottrina che, sorgendo da un dato sistema di forze storiche, vi resta inserita e vi opera dal di dentro. Ha quindi una forma correlativa alle contingenze di luogo e di tempo, ma ha insieme un contenuto ideale che la eleva a formula di verità nella storia superiore del pensiero. Non si agisce spiritualmente nel mondo come volontà umana dominatrice di volontà senza un concetto della realtà transeunte e particolare su cui bisogna agire, e della realtà permanente e universale in cui la prima ha il suo essere e la sua vita. Per conoscere gli uomini bisogna conoscere l'uomo; e per conoscere l'uomo bisogna conoscere la realtà e le sue leggi. Non c'è concetto dello stato che non sia fondamentalmente concetto della vita: filosofia o intuizione, sistema di idee che si svolge in una costruzione logica o si raccoglie in una visione o in una fede, ma è sempre, almeno virtualmente, una concezione organica del mondo.

II

Così il fascismo non si intenderebbe in molti dei suoi atteggiamenti pratici, come organizzazione di partito, come sistema di educazione, come disciplina, se non si guardasse alla luce del suo modo generale di concepire la vita. Modo spiritualistico. Il mondo per il fascismo non è questo mondo materiale che appare alla superficie, in cui l'uomo è un individuo separato da tutti gli altri e per sé stante, ed è governato da una legge naturale, che istintivamente lo trae a vivere una vita di piacere egoistico e momentaneo. L'uomo del fascismo è individuo che è nazione e patria, legge morale che stringe insieme individui e generazioni in una tradizione e in una missione, che sopprime l'istinto della vita chiusa nel breve giro del piacere per instaurare nel dovere una vita superiore libera da limiti di tempo e di spazio: una vita in cui l'individuo, attraverso l'abnegazione di sé, il sacrificio dei suoi interessi privati, la stessa morte, realizza quell'esistenza tutta spirituale in cui è il suo valore di uomo.

III

Dunque concezione spiritualistica, sorta anche essa dalla generale reazione del secolo contro il fiacco e materialistico positivismo dell'Ottocento. Antipositivistica, ma positiva: non scettica, né agnostica, né pessimistica, né passivamente ottimistica, come sono in generale le dottrine (tutte negative) che pongono il centro della vita fuori dell'uomo, che con la sua libera volontà può e deve crearsi il suo mondo. Il fascismo vuole l'uomo attivo e impegnato nell'azione con tutte le sue energie: lo vuole virilmente consapevole delle difficoltà che ci sono, e pronto ad affrontarle. Concepisce la vita come lotta pensando che spetti all'uomo conquistarsi quella che sia veramente degna di lui, creando prima di tutto in se stesso lo strumento (fisico, morale, intellettuale) per edificarla. Così per l'individuo singolo, così per la nazione, così per l'umanità. Quindi l'alto valore della cultura in tutte le sue forme (arte, religione, scienza) e l'importanza grandissima dell'educazione. Quindi anche il valore essenziale del lavoro, con cui l'uomo vince la natura e crea il mondo umano (economico, politico, morale, intellettuale).

IV

Questa concezione positiva della vita è evidentemente una concezione etica. E investe tutta la realtà, nonché l'attività umana che la signoreggia. Nessuna azione sottratta al giudizio morale; niente al mondo che si possa spogliare del valore che a tutto compete in ordine ai fini morali. La vita perciò quale la concepisce il fascista è seria, austera, religiosa: tutta librata in un mondo sorretto dalle forze morali e responsabili dello spirito. Il fascista disdegna la vita «comoda».

V

Il fascismo è una concezione religiosa, in cui l'uomo è visto nel suo immanente rapporto con una legge superiore, con una Volontà obiettiva che trascende l'individuo e lo eleva a membro consapevole di una società spirituale. Chi nella politica religiosa del regime fascista si è fermato a considerazioni di mera opportunità, non ha inteso che il fascismo, oltre a essere un sistema di governo, è anche, e prima di tutto, un sistema di pensiero.

VI

Il fascismo è una concezione storica, nella quale l'uomo non è quello che è se non in funzione del processo spirituale a cui concorre, nel gruppo familiare e sociale, nella nazione e nella storia, a cui tutte le nazioni collaborano. Donde il gran valore della tradizione nelle memorie, nella lingua, nei costumi, nelle norme del vivere sociale. Fuori della storia l'uomo è nulla. Perciò il fascismo è contro tutte le astrazioni individualistiche, a base materialistica, tipo sec. XVIII; ed è contro tutte le utopie e le innovazioni giacobine. Esso non crede possibile la «felicità» sulla terra come fu nel desiderio della letteratura economicistica del `700, e quindi respinge tutte le concezioni teleologiche per cui a un certo periodo della storia ci sarebbe una sistemazione definitiva del genere umano. Questo significa mettersi fuori della storia e della vita che è continuo fluire e divenire. Il fascismo politicamente vuol essere una dottrina realistica; praticamente, aspira a risolvere solo i problemi che si pongono storicamente da sé e che da sé trovano o suggeriscono la propria soluzione. Per agire tra gli uomini, come nella natura, bisogna entrare nel processo della realtà e impadronirsi delle forze in atto.

VII

Anti individualistica, la concezione fascista è per lo Stato; ed è per l'individuo in quanto esso coincide con lo Stato, coscienza e volontà universale dell'uomo nella sua esistenza storica. E' contro il liberalismo classico, che sorse dal bisogno di reagire all'assolutismo e ha esaurito la sua funzione storica da quando lo Stato si è trasformato nella stessa coscienza e volontà popolare. Il liberalismo negava lo Stato nell'interesse dell'individuo; il fascismo riafferma lo Stato come la realtà vera dell'individuo. E se la libertà dev'essere l'attributo dell'uomo reale, e non di quell'astratto fantoccio a cui pensava il liberalismo individualistico, il fascismo è per la libertà. È per la sola libertà che possa essere una cosa seria, la libertà dello Stato e dell'individuo nello Stato. Giacché, per il fascista, tutto è nello Stato, e nulla di umano o spirituale esiste, e tanto meno ha valore, fuori dello Stato. In tal senso il fascismo è totalitario, e lo Stato fascista, sintesi e unità di ogni valore, interpreta, sviluppa e potenzia tutta la vita del popolo.

VIII

Né individui fuori dello Stato, né gruppi (partiti politici, associazioni, sindacati, classi). Perciò il fascismo è contro il socialismo che irrigidisce il movimento storico nella lotta di classe e ignora l'unità statale che fonde le classi in una sola realtà economica e morale; e analogamente, è contro il sindacalismo classista. Ma nell'orbita dello Stato ordinatore, le reali esigenze da cui trasse origine il movimento socialista e sindacalista, il fascismo le vuole riconosciute e le fa valere nel sistema corporativo degli interessi conciliati nell'unità dello Stato.

IX

Gli individui sono classi secondo le categorie degli interessi; sono sindacati secondo le differenziate attività economiche cointeressate; ma sono prima di tutto e soprattutto Stato. Il quale non è numero, come somma d'individui formanti la maggioranza di un popolo. E perciò il fascismo è contro la democrazia che ragguaglia il popolo al maggior numero abbassandolo al livello dei più; ma è la forma più schietta di democrazia se il popolo è concepito, come dev'essere, qualitativamente e non quantitativamente, come l'idea più potente perché più morale, più coerente, più vera, che nel popolo si attua quale coscienza e volontà di pochi, anzi di Uno, e quale ideale tende ad attuarsi nella coscienza e volontà di tutti. Di tutti coloro che dalla natura e dalla storia, etnicamente, traggono ragione di formare una nazione, avviati sopra la stessa linea di sviluppo e formazione spirituale, come una coscienza e una volontà sola. Non razza, nè regione geograficamente individuata, ma generazione storicamente perpetuantesi, moltitudine unificata da un'idea, che è volontà di esistenza e di potenza: coscienza di sé, personalità.

X

Questa personalità superiore è bensì nazione in quanto è Stato. Non è la nazione a generare lo Stato, secondo l'obsoleto concetto naturalistico che servì di base alla pubblicistica degli Stati nazionali nel secolo XIX. Anzi la nazione è creata dallo Stato, che dà al popolo, consapevole della propria unità morale, una volontà, e quindi un'effettiva esistenza. Il diritto di una nazione all'indipendenza deriva non da una letteraria e ideale coscienza del proprio essere, e tanto meno da una situazione di fatto più o meno inconsapevole e inerte, ma da una coscienza attiva, da una volontà politica in atto e disposta a dimostrare il proprio diritto: cioè, da una sorta di Stato già in divenire. Lo Stato infatti, come volontà etica universale, è creatore del diritto.

XI

La nazione come Stato è una realtà etica che esiste e vive in quanto si sviluppa. Il suo arresto è la sua morte. Perciò lo Stato non solo è autorità che governa e dà forma di legge e valore di vita spirituale alle volontà individuali, ma è anche potenza che fa valere la sua volontà all'esterno, facendola riconoscere e rispettare, ossia dimostrandone col fatto l'universalità in tutte le determinazioni necessarie del suo svolgimento. È perciò organizzazione ed espansione, almeno virtuale. Cosi può adeguarsi alla natura dell'umana volontà, che nel suo sviluppo non conosce barriere, e che si realizza provando la propria infinità.

XII

Lo Stato fascista, forma più alta e potente della personalità, è forza, ma spirituale. La quale riassume tutte le forme della vita morale e intellettuale dell'uomo. Non si può quindi limitare a semplici funzioni di ordine e tutela, come voleva il liberalismo. Non è un semplice meccanismo che limiti la sfera delle presunte libertà individuali. È forma e norma interiore, disciplina di tutta la persona; penetra la volontà come l'intelligenza. Il suo principio, ispirazione centrale dell'umana personalità vivente nella comunità civile, scende nel profondo e si annida nel cuore dell'uomo d'azione come del pensatore, dell'artista come dello scienziato: anima dell'anima.

XIII

Il fascismo insomma non è soltanto datore di leggi e fondatore d'istituti, ma educatore e promotore di vita spirituale. Vuol rifare non le forme della vita umana, ma il contenuto, l'uomo, il carattere, la fede. E a questo fine vuole disciplina e autorità che scenda dentro gli spiriti, e vi domini incontrastata. La sua insegna perciò è il fascio littorio, simbolo dell'unità, della forza e della giustizia.

DOTTRINA POLITICA E SOCIALE

I

Quando, nell'ormai lontano marzo del 1919, dalle colonne del *Popolo d'Italia* convocai a Milano i superstiti interventisti-intervenuti, che mi avevano seguito sin dalla costituzione dei Fasci d'azione rivoluzionaria, avvenuta nel gennaio del 1915, non c'era nessuno specifico piano dottrinale nel mio spirito. Di una sola dottrina recavo l'esperienza vissuta: quella del socialismo dal 1903-04 sino all'inverno del 1914: circa un decennio. Esperienza di gregario e di capo, ma non esperienza dottrinale. La mia dottrina, anche in quel periodo, era stata la dottrina dell'azione. Una dottrina univoca e universalmente accettata del socialismo, non esisteva più sin dal 1905, quando cominciò in Germania il movimento revisionista facente capo a Eduard Bernstein e per contro si formò, nell'altalena delle tendenze, un movimento di sinistra rivoluzionario, che in Italia non uscì mai dal campo delle frasi, mentre, nel socialismo russo, fu il preludio del bolscevismo. Riformismo, rivoluzionarismo, centrismo, di questa terminologia anche gli echi sono spenti, mentre nel grande fiume del fascismo troverete i filoni che si dipartirono da Georges Sorel, da Hubert Lagardelle del *Mouvement Socialiste*, da Charles Péguy, e dalla coorte dei sindacalisti italiani, che tra il 1904 e il 1914 portarono una nota di novità nell'ambiente socialista italiano, già svirilizzato e cloroformizzato dalla fornicazione giolittiana, con le *Pagine libere* di Olivetti, *La Lupa* di Orano, il *Divenire sociale* di Enrico Leone. Nel 1919, finita la guerra, il socialismo era già morto come dottrina: esisteva solo come rancore, aveva ancora una sola possibilità, specialmente in Italia, la rappresaglia contro coloro che avevano voluto la guerra e che dovevano espiarla. Il *Popolo d'Italia* recava nel sottotitolo «quotidiano dei combattenti e dei produttori». La parola «produttori» era già l'espressione di un indirizzo mentale. Il fascismo non fu tenuto a balia da una dottrina elaborata in precedenza, a tavolino: nacque da un bisogno di azione e fu azione; non fu partito, ma, nei primi due anni, antipartito e movimento. Il nome che io diedi all'organizzazione, ne fissava i caratteri. Eppure chi rilegga, nei fogli ormai sgualciti dell'epoca, il resoconto dell'adunata costitutiva dei Fasci italiani di combattimento, non troverà una dottrina, ma una serie di spunti, di anticipazioni, di accenni, che, liberati dall'inevitabile ganga delle contingenze, dovevano poi, dopo alcuni anni, svilupparsi in una serie di posizioni dottrinali, che facevano del fascismo una dottrina politica a sé stante, in confronto di tutte le altre, passate e contemporanee. «Se la borghesia, dicevo allora, crede di trovare in noi dei parafulmini si inganna. Noi dobbiamo andare incontro al lavoro... Vogliamo abituare le classi operaie alla capacità direttiva, anche per convincerle che non è facile mandare avanti una industria o un commercio... Combatteremo il retroguardismo tecnico e spirituale... Aperta la successione del regime noi non dobbiamo essere degli imbelli. Dobbiamo correre; se il regime sarà superato saremo noi che dovremo occupare il suo posto. Il diritto di successione ci viene perché spingemmo il paese alla guerra e lo conducemmo alla vittoria. L'attuale rappresentanza politica non ci può bastare, vogliamo una rappresentanza diretta dei singoli interessi... Si potrebbe dire contro questo programma che si ritorna alle corporazioni. Non importa!... Vorrei perciò che l'assemblea accettasse le rivendicazioni del sindacalismo nazionale dal punto di vista economico»... Non è singolare che sin dalla prima giornata di Piazza San Sepolcro risuoni la parola «corporazione» che doveva, nel corso della Rivoluzione, significare una delle creazioni legislative e sociali alla base del regime?

II

Gli anni che precedettero la marcia su Roma, furono anni durante i quali le necessità dell'azione non tollerarono indagini o complete elaborazioni dottrinali. Si battagliava nelle città e nei villaggi. Si discuteva, ma quel ch'è più sacro e importante, si moriva. Si sapeva morire. La dottrina bell'e formata, con divisione di capitoli e paragrafi e contorno di elucubrazioni, poteva mancare; ma c'era a sostituirla qualcosa di più decisivo: la fede. Purtuttavia, a chi rimemori sulla scorta dei libri, degli articoli, dei voti dei congressi, dei discorsi maggiori e minori, chi sappia indagare e scegliere, troverà che i fondamenti della dottrina furono gettati mentre infuriava la battaglia. È precisamente in quegli anni che anche il pensiero fascista si arma, si raffina, procede verso una sua organizzazione. I problemi dell'individuo e dello Stato; i problemi dell'autorità e della libertà; i problemi politici e sociali e quelli più specificatamente nazionali; la lotta contro le dottrine liberali, democratiche, socialistiche, massoniche, popolaresche fu condotta contemporaneamente alle «spedizioni punitive». Ma poiché mancò il «sistema» si negò dagli avversari in malafede al fascismo ogni capacità di dottrina, mentre la dottrina veniva sorgendo, sia pure tumultuosamente dapprima sotto l'aspetto di una negazione violenta e dogmatica come accade di tutte le idee che esordiscono, poi sotto l'aspetto positivo di una costruzione che trovava, successivamente negli anni 1926, `27 e `28, la sua realizzazione nelle leggi e negli istituti del regime. Il fascismo è oggi nettamente individuato non solo come regime ma come dottrina. Questa parola va interpretata nel senso che oggi il fascismo esercitando la sua critica su se stesso e sugli altri, ha un suo proprio inconfondibile punto di vista, di riferimento e quindi di direzione, dinnanzi a tutti i problemi che angustiano, nelle cose o nelle intelligenze, i popoli del mondo.

III

Anzitutto il fascismo, per quanto riguarda, in generale, l'avvenire e lo sviluppo dell'umanità, e a parte ogni considerazione di politica attuale, non crede alla possibilità né all'utilità della pace perpetua. Respinge quindi il pacifismo che nasconde una rinuncia alla lotta e una viltà di fronte al sacrificio. Solo la guerra porta alla massima tensione tutte le energie umane e imprime un sigillo di nobiltà ai popoli che hanno la virtù di affrontarla. Tutte le altre prove sono dei sostituti, che non pongono mai l'uomo di fronte a se stesso, nell'alternativa della vita e della morte.

Una dottrina, quindi, che parta dal postulato pregiudiziale della pace, è estranea al fascismo così come estranee allo spirito del fascismo, anche se accettate per quel tanto di utilità che possano avere in determinate situazioni politiche, sono tutte le costruzioni internazionalistiche e societarie, le quali, come la storia dimostra, si possono disperdere al vento quando elementi sentimentali, ideali e pratici muovono a tempesta il cuore dei popoli

Questo spirito anti-pacifista, il fascismo lo trasporta anche nella vita degli individui. L'orgoglioso motto squadrista «me ne frego», scritto sulle bende di una ferita, è un atto di filosofia non soltanto stoica, è il sunto di una dottrina non soltanto politica: è l'educazione al combattimento, l'accettazione dei rischi che esso comporta; è un nuovo stile di vita italiano. Così il fascista accetta, ama la vita, ignora e ritiene vile il suicidio; comprende la vita come dovere, elevazione, conquista: la vita che deve essere alta e piena: vissuta per sè, ma soprattutto per gli altri, vicini e lontani, presenti e futuri.

IV

La politica demografica del regime è la conseguenza di queste premesse. Anche il fascista ama infatti il suo prossimo, ma questo prossimo non è per lui un concetto vago e inafferrabile: l'amore per il prossimo non impedisce le necessarie educatrici severità, e ancora meno le differenziazioni e le distanze. Il fascismo respinge gli abbracciamenti universali e, pur vivendo nella comunità dei popoli civili, li guarda vigilante e diffidente negli occhi, li segue nei loro stati d'animo e nella trasformazione dei loro interessi né si lascia ingannare da apparenze mutevoli e fallaci.

V

Una siffatta concezione della vita porta il fascismo a essere la negazione recisa di quella dottrina che costituì la base del socialismo cosiddetto scientifico o marxiano: la dottrina del materialismo storico secondo il quale la storia delle civiltà umane si spiegherebbe soltanto con la lotta d'interessi fra i diversi gruppi sociali e col cambiamento dei mezzi e strumenti di produzione. Che le vicende dell'economia come le scoperte di materie prime, nuovi metodi di lavoro, invenzioni scientifiche abbiano una loro importanza, nessuno nega; ma che esse bastino a spiegare la storia umana escludendone tutti gli altri fattori, è assurdo: il fascismo crede ancora e sempre nella santità e nell'eroismo, cioè in atti nei quali nessun motivo economico, lontano o vicino, agisce. Negato il materialismo storico, per cui gli uomini non sarebbero che comparse della storia, che appaiono e scompaiono alla superficie dei flutti, mentre nel profondo si agitano e lavorano le vere forze direttrici, è negata anche la lotta di classe, immutabile e irreparabile, che di questa concezione economicistica della storia è la naturale figliazione, e soprattutto è negato che la lotta di classe sia l'agente preponderante delle trasformazioni sociali. Colpito il socialismo in questi due capisaldi della sua dottrina, di esso non resta allora che l'aspirazione sentimentale, antica come l'umanità, a una convivenza sociale nella quale siano alleviate le sofferenze e i dolori della più umile gente. Ma qui il fascismo respinge il concetto di «felicità» economica, che si realizzerebbe socialisticamente e quasi automaticamente a un dato momento dell'evoluzione dell'economia, con l'assicurare a tutti il massimo benessere. Il fascismo nega il concetto materialistico di «felicità» come possibile e lo abbandona agli economisti della prima metà del `700; nega cioè l'equazione benessere=felicità che convertirebbe gli uomini in animali di una cosa sola pensosi: quella di essere pasciuti e ingrassati, ridotti, quindi, alla pura e semplice vita vegetativa.

VI

Dopo il socialismo, il fascismo batte in breccia tutto il complesso delle ideologie democratiche e le respinge, sia nelle loro premesse teoriche, sia nelle loro applicazioni o strumentazioni pratiche. Il fascismo nega che il numero, per il semplice fatto di essere numero, possa dirigere le società umane; nega che questo numero possa governare attraverso una consultazione periodica; afferma la disuguaglianza irrimediabile e feconda e benefica degli uomini che non si possono livellare attraverso un fatto meccanico ed estrinseco com'è il suffragio universale. Regimi democratici possono essere definiti quelli nei quali, di tanto in tanto, si dà al popolo l'illusione di essere sovrano, mentre la vera effettiva sovranità sta in altre forze talora irresponsabili e segrete. La democrazia è un regime senza re, ma con moltissimi re talora più esclusivi, tirannici e rovinosi che un solo re che sia tiranno. Questo spiega perché il fascismo, pur avendo prima del 1922 per ragioni di contingenza assunto un atteggiamento di tendenzialità repubblicana, vi rinunciò prima della marcia su Roma, convinto che la questione delle forme politiche di uno Stato non è, oggi, preminente e che studiando nel campionario delle monarchie passate e presenti, delle repubbliche passate e presenti, risulta che monarchia e repubblica non sono da giudicare sotto la specie dell'eternità, ma rappresentano forme nelle quali si estrinseca l'evoluzione politica, la storia, la tradizione, la psicologia di un determinato paese. Ora il fascismo supera l'antitesi monarchia-repubblica sulla quale si attardò il democraticismo, caricando la prima di tutte le insufficienze, e apologizzando l'ultima come regime di perfezione. Ora s'è visto che ci sono repubbliche intimamente reazionarie o assolutistiche, e monarchie che accolgono le più ardite esperienze politiche e sociali.

VII

«La ragione, la scienza - diceva Ernest Renan, che ebbe delle illuminazioni prefasciste, in una delle sue Meditazioni filosofiche - sono dei prodotti dell'umanità, ma volere la ragione direttamente per il popolo e attraverso il popolo è una chimera. Non è necessario per l'esistenza della ragione che tutto il mondo la conosca. In ogni caso se tale iniziazione dovesse farsi non si farebbe attraverso la bassa democrazia, che sembra dover condurre all'estinzione di ogni cultura difficile, e di ogni più alta disciplina. Il principio che la società esiste solo per il benessere e la libertà degli individui che la compongono non sembra essere conforme ai piani della natura, piani nei quali la specie sola è presa in considerazione e l'individuo sembra sacrificato. È da temere fortemente che l'ultima parola della democrazia così intesa (mi affretto a dire che si può intendere anche diversamente) non sia uno stato sociale nel quale una massa degenerata non avrebbe altra preoccupazione che godere i piaceri ignobili dell'uomo volgare». Fin qui Renan. Il fascismo respinge nella democrazia l'assurda menzogna convenzionale dell'egalitarismo politico e l'abito dell'irresponsabilità collettiva e il mito della felicità e del progresso indefinito. Ma, se la democrazia può essere diversamente intesa, cioè se democrazia significa non respingere il popolo ai margini dello Stato, il fascismo poté da chi scrive essere definito una «democrazia organizzata, centralizzata, autoritaria».

VIII

Di fronte alle dottrine liberali, il fascismo è in atteggiamento di assoluta opposizione, sia nel campo della politica sia in quello dell'economia. Non bisogna esagerare, a scopi semplicemente di polemica attuale, l'importanza del liberalismo nel secolo scorso, e fare di quella che fu una delle numerose dottrine sbocciate in quel secolo, una religione dell'umanità per tutti i tempi presenti e futuri. Il liberalismo non fiorì che per un quindicennio. Nacque nel 1830 come reazione alla Santa Alleanza che voleva respingere l'Europa al pre-'89, ed ebbe il suo anno di splendore nel 1848 quando anche Pio IX fu liberale. Subito dopo cominciò la decadenza. Se il '48 fu un anno di luce e di poesia, il '49 fu un anno di tenebre e di tragedia. La repubblica di Roma fu uccisa da un'altra repubblica, quella di Francia. Nello stesso anno, Marx lanciava il vangelo della religione del socialismo, col famoso Manifesto dei comunisti. Nel 1851 Napoleone III fa il suo illiberale colpo di Stato e regna sulla Francia fino al 1870, quando fu rovesciato da un moto di popolo, ma in seguito a una disfatta militare fra le più grandi che conti la storia. Il vittorioso è Bismarck, il quale non seppe mai dove stesse di casa la religione della libertà e di quali profeti si servisse. È sintomatico che un popolo di alta civiltà, come il popolo tedesco, abbia ignorato in pieno, per tutto il sec. XIX, la religione della libertà. Non c'è che una parentesi. Rappresentata da quello che è stato chiamato il «ridicolo parlamento di Francoforte», che durò una stagione. La Germania ha raggiunto la sua unità nazionale al di fuori del liberalismo, contro il liberalismo, dottrina che sembra estranea all'anima tedesca, anima essenzialmente monarchica, mentre il liberalismo è l'anticamera storica e logica dell'anarchia. Le tappe dell'unità tedesca sono le tre guerre del `64, `66, `70, guidate da «liberali» come Moltke e Bismarck. Quanto all'unità italiana, il liberalismo vi ha avuto una parte assolutamente inferiore all'apporto dato da Mazzini e da Garibaldi che liberali non furono. Senza l'intervento dell'illiberale Napoleone, non avremmo avuto la Lombardia, e senza l'aiuto dell'illiberale Bismarck a Sadowa e a Sedan, molto probabilmente non avremmo avuto, nel `66, la Venezia; e nel 1870 non saremmo entrati a Roma. Dal 1870 al 1915, corre il periodo nel quale gli stessi sacerdoti del nuovo credo accusano il crepuscolo della loro religione: battuta in breccia dal decadentismo nella letteratura, dall'attivismo nella pratica. Attivismo: cioè nazionalismo, futurismo, fascismo. Il secolo «liberale» dopo aver accumulato un'infinità di nodi gordiani, cerca di scioglierli con l'ecatombe della guerra mondiale. Mai nessuna religione impose così immane sacrificio. Gli dei del liberalismo avevano sete di sangue? Ora il liberalismo sta per chiudere le porte dei suoi templi deserti perché i popoli sentono che il suo agnosticismo nell'economia, il suo indifferentismo nella politica e nella morale condurrebbe, come ha condotto, a sicura rovina gli Stati. Si spiega con ciò che tutte le esperienze politiche del mondo contemporaneo sono antiliberali ed è supremamente ridicolo volerle perciò classificare fuori della storia; come se la storia fosse una bandita di caccia riservata al liberalismo e ai suoi professori, come se il liberalismo fosse la parola definitiva e non più superabile della civiltà.

IX

Le negazioni fasciste del socialismo, della democrazia, del liberalismo, non devono tuttavia far credere che il fascismo voglia respingere il mondo a quello che era prima di quel 1789, che viene indicato come l'anno di apertura del secolo demo-liberale. Non si torna indietro. La dottrina fascista non ha eletto a suo profeta De Maistre. L'assolutismo monarchico *fu*, e così pure ogni ecclesiolatria. E così *furono* i privilegi feudali e la divisione in caste impenetrabili e non comunicabili fra di loro.

Il concetto di autorità fascista non ha niente a che vedere con lo stato di polizia. Un partito che governa totalitariamente una nazione, è un fatto nuovo nella storia. Non sono possibili riferimenti e confronti. Il fascismo dalle macerie delle dottrine liberali, socialistiche, democratiche, trae quegli elementi che hanno ancora un valore di vita. Mantiene quelli che si potrebbero dire i fatti acquisiti della storia, respinge tutto il resto, cioè il concetto di una dottrina buona per tutti i tempi e per tutti i popoli. Ammesso che il sec. XIX sia stato il secolo del socialismo, del liberalismo, della democrazia, non è detto che anche il sec. XX debba essere il secolo del socialismo, del liberalismo, della democrazia. Le dottrine politiche passano, i popoli restano. Si può pensare che questo sia il secolo dell'autorità, un secolo di destra, un secolo fascista; se il XIX fu il secolo dell'individuo (liberalismo significa individualismo), si può pensare che questo sia il secolo collettivo e quindi il secolo dello Stato. Che una nuova dottrina possa utilizzare gli elementi ancora vitali di altre dottrine è perfettamente logico. Nessuna dottrina nacque tutta nuova, lucente, mai vista. Nessuna dottrina può vantare una originalità assoluta. Essa è legata, non fosse che storicamente, alle altre dottrine che furono, alle altre dottrine che saranno. Così il socialismo scientifico di Marx è legato al socialismo utopistico dei Fourier, degli Owen, dei Saint-Simon; così il liberalismo dell'800 si riattacca a tutto il movimento illuministico del `700. Così le dottrine democratiche sono legate all'Enciclopedia. Ogni dottrina tende a indirizzare l'attività degli uomini verso un determinato obiettivo; ma l'attività degli uomini reagisce sulla dottrina, la trasforma, l'adatta alle nuove necessità o la supera. La dottrina quindi, dev'essere essa stessa non un'esercitazione di parole, ma un atto di vita. In ciò le venature pragmatistiche del fascismo, la sua volontà di potenza, il suo volere essere, la sua posizione di fronte al fatto «violenza» e al suo valore.

X

Caposaldo della dottrina fascista è la concezione dello Stato, della sua essenza, dei suoi compiti, delle sue finalità. Per il fascismo lo Stato è un assoluto, davanti al quale individui e gruppi sono il relativo. Individui e gruppi sono «pensabili» in quanto siano nello Stato. Lo Stato liberale non dirige il gioco e lo sviluppo materiale e spirituale delle collettività, ma si limita a registrare i risultati; lo Stato fascista ha una sua consapevolezza, una sua volontà, per questo si chiama uno Stato «etico».

Nel 1929 alla prima assemblea quinquennale del regime io dicevo: «Per il fascismo lo Stato non è il guardiano notturno che si occupa soltanto della sicurezza personale dei cittadini; non è nemmeno una organizzazione a fini puramente materiali, come quello di garantire un certo benessere e una relativa pacifica convivenza sociale, nel qual caso a realizzarlo basterebbe un consiglio di amministrazione; non è nemmeno una creazione di politica pura, senza aderenze con la realtà materiale e complessa della vita dei singoli e di quella dei popoli. Lo Stato così come il fascismo lo concepisce e attua è un fatto spirituale e morale, poiché concreta l'organizzazione politica, giuridica, economica della nazione, e tale organizzazione è, nel suo sorgere e nel suo sviluppo, una manifestazione dello spirito. Lo Stato è garante della sicurezza interna ed esterna, ma è anche il custode e il trasmettitore dello spirito del popolo così come fu nei secoli elaborato nella lingua, nel costume, nella fede. Lo Stato non è soltanto presente, ma è anche passato e soprattutto futuro. È lo Stato che trascendendo il limite breve delle vite individuali rappresenta la coscienza immanente della nazione. Le forme in cui gli Stati si esprimono, mutano, ma la necessità rimane. È lo Stato che educa i cittadini alla virtù civile, li rende consapevoli della loro missione, li sollecita all'unità; armonizza i loro interessi nella giustizia; tramanda le conquiste del pensiero nelle scienze, nelle arti, nel diritto, nell'umana solidarietà; porta gli uomini dalla vita elementare della tribù alla più alta espressione umana di potenza che è l'impero; affida ai secoli i nomi di coloro che morirono per la sua integrità o per obbedire alle sue leggi; addita come esempio e raccomanda alle generazioni che verranno, i capitani che lo accrebbero di territorio e i genii che lo illuminarono di gloria. Quando declina il senso dello Stato e prevalgono le tendenze dissociatrici e centrifughe degli individui o dei gruppi, le società nazionali volgono al tramonto».

XI

Dal 1929 a oggi, l'evoluzione economica politica universale ha ancora rafforzato queste posizioni dottrinali. Chi giganteggia è lo Stato. Chi può risolvere le drammatiche contraddizioni del capitalismo è lo Stato. Quella che si chiama crisi, non si può risolvere se non dallo Stato, entro lo Stato. Dove sono le ombre dei Jules Simon, che agli albori del liberalismo proclamavano che «lo Stato deve lavorare a rendersi inutile e a preparare le sue dimissioni»? Dei Mac Culloch, che nella seconda metà del secolo scorso affermavano che lo Stato deve astenersi dal troppo governare? E che cosa direbbe mai dinnanzi ai continui, sollecitati, inevitabili interventi dello Stato nelle vicende economiche, Jeremy Bentham, secondo il quale l'industria avrebbe dovuto chiedere allo Stato soltanto di essere lasciata in pace, o il tedesco Humboldt, secondo il quale lo Stato «ozioso» doveva essere considerato il migliore? Vero è che la seconda ondata degli economisti liberali fu meno estremista della prima e già lo stesso Adam Smith apriva (sia pure cautamente) la porta agli interventi dello Stato nell'economia. Se chi dice liberalismo dice individuo, chi dice fascismo dice Stato. Ma lo Stato fascista è unico ed è una creazione originale. Non è reazionario, ma rivoluzionario, in quanto anticipa le soluzioni di determinati problemi universali quali sono posti altrove nel campo politico dal frazionamento dei partiti, dal prepotere del parlamentarismo, dall'irresponsabilità delle assemblee; nel campo economico dalle funzioni sindacali sempre più numerose e potenti sia nel settore operaio come in quello industriale, dai loro conflitti e dalle loro intese; nel campo morale dalla necessità dell'ordine, della disciplina, dell'obbedienza a quelli che sono i dettami morali della patria. Il fascismo vuole lo Stato forte, organico e al tempo stesso poggiato su una larga base popolare. Lo Stato fascista ha rivendicato a sé anche il campo dell'economia e, attraverso le istituzioni corporative, sociali, educative da lui create, il senso dello Stato arriva sino alle estreme propaggini, e nello Stato circolano, inquadrate nelle rispettive organizzazioni, tutte le forze politiche, economiche, spirituali della nazione. Uno Stato che poggia su milioni d'individui che lo riconoscono, lo sentono, sono pronti a servirlo, non è lo Stato tirannico del signore medievale. Non ha niente di comune con gli Stati assolutistici di prima o dopo l'89. L'individuo nello Stato fascista non è annullato, ma piuttosto moltiplicato, così come in un reggimento un soldato non è diminuito, ma moltiplicato per il numero dei suoi camerati. Lo Stato fascista organizza la nazione, ma lascia poi agli individui margini sufficienti; esso ha limitato le libertà inutili o nocive e ha conservato quelle essenziali. Chi giudica su questo terreno non può essere l'individuo, ma soltanto lo Stato.

XII

Lo Stato fascista non rimane indifferente di fronte al fatto religioso in genere e a quella particolare religione positiva che è il cattolicismo italiano. Lo Stato non ha una teologia, ma ha una morale. Nello Stato fascista la religione viene considerata come una delle manifestazioni più profonde dello spirito; non viene, quindi, soltanto rispettata, ma difesa e protetta. Lo Stato fascista non crea un suo Dio così come volle fare a un certo momento, nei deliri estremi della Convenzione, Robespierre; né cerca vanamente di cancellarlo dagli animi come fa il bolscevismo; il fascismo rispetta il Dio degli asceti, dei santi, degli eroi e anche il Dio così come visto e pregato dal cuore ingenuo e primitivo del popolo.

XIII

Lo Stato fascista è una volontà di potenza e d'imperio. La tradizione romana è qui un'idea di forza. Nella dottrina del fascismo l'impero non è soltanto un'espressione territoriale o militare o mercantile, ma spirituale o morale. Si può pensare a un impero, cioè a una nazione che direttamente o indirettamente guida altre nazioni, senza bisogno di conquistare un solo chilometro quadrato di territorio. Per il fascismo la tendenza all'impero, cioè all'espansione delle nazioni, è una manifestazione di vitalità; il suo contrario, o il piede di casa, è un segno di decadenza: popoli che sorgono o risorgono sono imperialisti, popoli che muoiono sono rinunciatari. Il fascismo è la dottrina più adeguata a rappresentare le tendenze, gli stati d'animo di un popolo come l'italiano che risorge dopo molti secoli di abbandono o di servitù straniera. Ma l'impero chiede disciplina, coordinazione degli sforzi, dovere e sacrificio; questo spiega molti aspetti dell'azione pratica del regime e l'indirizzo di molte forze dello Stato e la severità necessaria contro coloro che vorrebbero opporsi a questo moto spontaneo e fatale dell'Italia nel secolo XX, e opporsi agitando le ideologie superate del secolo XIX, ripudiate dovunque si siano osati grandi esperimenti di trasformazioni politiche e sociali: non mai come in questo momento i popoli hanno avuto sete di autorità, di direttive, di ordine. Se ogni secolo ha una sua dottrina, da mille indizi appare che quella del secolo attuale è il fascismo. Che sia una dottrina di vita, lo mostra il fatto che ha suscitato una fede: che la fede abbia conquistato le anime, lo dimostra il fatto che il fascismo ha avuto i suoi caduti e i suoi martiri. Il fascismo ha oramai nel mondo l'universalità di tutte le dottrine che, realizzandosi, rappresentano un momento nella storia dello spirito umano.

Milton Keynes UK
Ingram Content Group UK Ltd.
UKHW020101050824
446426UK00013B/249

From Darkness to Light

From Darkness to Light

Charles Miles

XULON PRESS

Xulon Press
555 Winderley Pl, Suite 225
Maitland, FL 32751
407.339.4217
www.xulonpress.com

© 2024 by Charles Miles

All rights reserved solely by the author. The author guarantees all contents are original and do not infringe upon the legal rights of any other person or work. No part of this book may be reproduced in any form without the permission of the author.

Due to the changing nature of the Internet, if there are any web addresses, links, or URLs included in this manuscript, these may have been altered and may no longer be accessible. The views and opinions shared in this book belong solely to the author and do not necessarily reflect those of the publisher. The publisher therefore disclaims responsibility for the views or opinions expressed within the work.

Unless otherwise indicated, Scripture quotations taken from the King James Version (KJV) – public domain.
Scripture quotations taken from the Holy Bible, New International Version (NIV). Copyright © 1973, 1978, 1984, 2011 by Biblica, Inc.™. Used by permission. All rights reserved.

Paperback ISBN-13: 978-1-66289-955-3
Ebook ISBN-13: 978-1-66289-956-0

While writing this book, I had to truly introspect, delving into my life to decide what I wanted people to know about my past. My aim is to expose and educate readers about the dangers of the occult without glorifying it. I intend to illustrate my personal journey from darkness to light, hoping that this narrative will lead people to Jesus. For those who already know Jesus as their personal savior, I aim to enlighten them about how the enemy can infiltrate their lives.

Although this won't be a lengthy book, I trust that you will find it informative. My goal is to encourage readers to carefully consider the paths they choose and recognize the potential consequences. I understand that people will ultimately do as they please, but my desire is to show them that there are consequences to their actions.

Referencing God's Word, in the book of Hosea (Chapter 4, Verse 6), it states: "My people are destroyed from the lack of knowledge. Because you have rejected knowledge, I also reject you as my priests; because you have ignored the law of your God. I will also ignore your children." Additionally, James (Chapter 1, Verse 5) advises, "If any of you lacks wisdom, you should ask God, who gives generously to all without fault, and it will be given to you." Through writing this book, I aim to equip readers with knowledge and, if lacking, wisdom. Beyond mere enjoyment, my greater goal is for readers to be educated and gain the knowledge that many people seem to lack, especially within churches where deception by the enemy is prevalent.

Drawing from 2 Corinthians (Chapter 6, Verse 17), which urges believers to "come out among the unbelievers and separate yourself from them," I emphasize the importance of avoiding contamination and compromise. God's instruction is clear: don't engage with those who will pollute you.

I hope that as you read this book, you are touched by God, and I pray that you learn valuable lessons from it. This marks my first attempt at writing a book, a venture born out of obedience to God. It underscores the importance of prioritizing Jesus' desires over our own. Making Jesus the Lord of our lives means allowing Him to be God in every aspect.

Reflecting on our time in the world, we often fail when attempting things on our own. Jesus loves you and desires the best for your life. Though unsure of what Jesus is calling you to do, it is crucial to obey His commands. Stepping out in faith will pave the way, regardless of circumstances. Trust in what He says, be obedient, and leave the rest to God.

In closing, I offer this prayer: "Dear Jesus, I thank you for allowing me to serve you obediently. I pray that this book, created out of love, touches readers' hearts, leading them to seek you with joy and humility. May they be obedient to you, getting to know you more. In Jesus' name, Amen."

Dedication

I want to thank my Lord and Savior, Jesus Christ, for all the wonderful things that He is doing in my life and for giving me the courage to write this book. The day that I gave my life to Jesus is the day my life began. Even when trials come my way, I know He is always there and will see me through.

I want to thank my wonderful wife, Violet, for supporting me on this book. I appreciate and love you more than you will know.

I hope everyone who reads this book will be touched and will change their lives through Jesus, our Lord and Savior.

Table of Contents

1 My Involvement in the Occult .1

2 Coming to Jesus. 9

3 Warning to Parents 13

4 What We as Christians Need to Do 21

1
My Involvement in the Occult

When I was a teenager, I started out in the occult with the Ouija board and Dungeons and Dragons. I was in middle school when I became attracted to these things. I was in middle school in the 1980s, and it was the time of the big hair bands, which I was into. I was never popular and did not fit in, and there was not much difference in high school. When I started high school, I moved from upstate New York to San Diego. I went to one high school for half of a semester, then moved and started another high school. I was still into Dungeon and Dragons and then ventured out into other occult practices. My mom was a single mom; my parents got divorced when I was in New York, and my father was never around. I have very few memories of my father.

Most of my memories involve my father taking me to different bars and getting drunk most of the time. My mother was not around much due to her constant work to support us. She tried to provide my sister and me with the basics, as my father never contributed financially. In junior high school, I excelled in karate, becoming very proficient. Through karate, I was introduced to Eastern philosophy.

Despite my achievements, I had few friends in junior high. Moving to San Diego made it even more challenging to make friends, and just when connections started forming, we had to move again, restarting the process. The friends I made were fellow socially awkward teenagers, considered misfits. We were not good at gym, couldn't get a date, and were placed in special classes for people with dyslexia. While I consistently received good grades, I always sought a place to fit in.

In search of belonging, I explored different religions and tried various churches but felt rejected for asking questions about the Bible. Upon starting community college, I embraced Satanism, following Anton LaVey's teachings, believing it was the right fit at the time. I delved into the Satanic Bible and couldn't get enough, but I eventually realized it wasn't the right path. I decided to give church another chance, only to feel rejected once more.

Turning to Wicca, I found a local Druidic grove in San Diego, where I became an elder, teaching newcomers and serving on the local council. Despite my involvement, very few in the Pagan community knew me as a person. Engaging in various occult practices such as divination,

My Involvement in the Occult

astral projection, spells, and curses, I read works by occult authors, including Aleister Crowley.

I attended many pagan events, participating in rituals and taking various occult classes. Eager to learn new practices, I traveled extensively, from my home in San Diego to Tijuana, Mexico, San Jose, Long Beach, Los Angeles, and Boston for rituals and classes. In my San Diego home, I used a scrying mirror, often encountering spirits. During a Druid ritual, we performed a guided meditation involving astral projection, collectively visiting Helheim (Hel), part of Norse culture.

In Norse culture, Hel was a place one went after death if they did not die a glorious death. When our group visited Hell during a guided meditation, we were deceived by a devil figure into believing it was a glorious place. Unfortunately, we didn't get to see what Hell truly is, and I, having been there before, looked forward to returning.

At that time, my wife and I were deeply involved in occult practices, attending many rituals together. In San Diego, we played a role in introducing Spiral Scouts to the Pagan community, an endeavor that continues to teach children today. I attended rituals on my own during our separation. We raised our two sons in Paganism, but as the oldest entered high school, he became interested in Satanism, and I bought him the Satanic Bible. Both sons embraced heavy metal music, seemingly following in my footsteps.

My ex-wife and I, separated numerous times and divorced twice, attended Druid rituals where she performed Aztec rituals. During parts of our marriage, a lesbian couple lived with us, and our home always had a variety of alcoholic beverages. Alcohol was offered as a sacrifice during Druid rituals to our gods, goddesses, and ancestors, with many members partaking. Camping trips involved full days of classes, followed by nighttime rituals and heavy drinking around a bonfire, sometimes with marijuana present. We taught the children pagan ways, attending events like Witch's Night Out (a Samhain event) and Pagan Pride, where diverse communities participated.

I attended Wiccan events where a lesbian couple ran one coven, and another was led by a high priestess who was a dominatrix with her female sex slave and husband present. In the pagan community, the normalization of magick and homosexuality was prevalent. When my oldest son showed interest in Satanism, I supported him by buying the Satanic Bible and their preferred heavy metal music. Looking back, I realize my approach may have been misguided.

Having married and divorced my ex-wife twice and faced numerous separations, my current relationship began on a pagan dating site. My current wife was into Hinduism, while I was deeply immersed in the Celtic and Irish cultures. Our wedding in San Diego, conducted by a dominatrix high priestess with her sex slave present, involved a handfasting ceremony with a rope over our hands symbolizing unity, followed by jumping over a broomstick to signify transitioning from single to married life. The celebration included a significant amount of alcohol, and during that period, I relied heavily on alcohol as an escape, often finding solace in tears before falling asleep. Despite the outward appearance of happiness, many times, it was merely an act.

I would often have many people around me, yet I felt very lonely because they did not know the real me. Many would want to be around me, but I constantly questioned whether it was for who I truly was or the facade I presented. Most of the time, I was uncertain about who my real friends were. I became skilled at masking my true feelings, often lying to others and deceiving myself about my emotions. During this phase of my life, thoughts of suicide crossed my mind as a way to escape the pain I felt.

We observed all the Sabbaths (high days), including Samhain, also known as Halloween, during which many members of the pagan community, myself included, would cast curses over candy and costumes. This was driven by a sense of disrespect felt towards outsiders celebrating our holiday and appropriating our sacred day. The curses often targeted disobedience in children and predicted relationship troubles for both adults and children.

Many people are unaware of the reasons behind certain holiday traditions, such as carving pumpkins. The practice originated from an Irish story about Stingy Jack, a drunkard who outsmarted Satan twice, leading to his wandering the Earth with an amber from Hell in a turnip lantern. The tradition evolved into carving pumpkins in the United States, with people often oblivious to its darker origins.

Halloween, in particular, is viewed negatively due to its association with opening doors to the dark side and welcoming demons. The author advises against celebrating it and urges churches and Christians to avoid any involvement. There is a strong stance against parents allowing their children to partake in Halloween, believing it exposes them to demonic influences.

During a ritual in San Diego at the beach, I took an oath and was baptized into a Druid group in the mid 2000. In July 2019, my wife and I moved to Charleston, South Carolina, where I received permission to start a local group, a proto-grove named the Local Proto-grove. I organized rituals in the park, connected with local pagans, and promoted our version of Paganism.

This is where we get the tradition of carving pumpkins as Jack o' lanterns. This is not a good story, and people are often unaware of why they carve pumpkins. When the Irish were in Ireland, they carved turnips. Still, when they came to the United States, they started carving pumpkins because it was easier and more substantial. People wear costumes without understanding the reasons behind this, often thinking it's all just fun and games. However, celebrating Halloween opens doors to the dark side, to demons, and many do so without realizing the potential consequences. Churches and Christians should avoid any part of this day, as attempting to turn something inherently evil into something good is futile.

Parents should refrain from saying they don't want their children to miss out on Halloween, as the question arises: What are your children missing out on, being potentially tormented by demons? It's unlikely that they will want to spend time with Jesus or the Word of God in such circumstances. Some things in life should be avoided, and the author expresses that they don't need a specific day to get candy since stores sell it year-round, and they already have candy at home.

During one of the rituals in San Diego, which took place at the beach, I gave an oath and was baptized into the Druid group. In July 2019, I moved with my wife from San Diego to Charleston, South Carolina. Upon arrival, I was given permission to start a local group, a proto-grove named the Local Proto-grove, listed with rituals in the park. I encountered challenges as the founder of the organization, who was involved in child molestation when alive, became known to me and others. This information made promoting the group difficult. People I never met contacted me about joining the proto-grove, prompting explanations over the phone about our beliefs and how to join.

However, the onset of COVID-19 made having rituals almost impossible. Additionally, conflicts with the neighbors led me to use magic to curse them, employing candle magic, war water, and placing names in bottles. My wife and I performed protection spells to keep them away from us. Due to the stress and our actions, my wife was hospitalized multiple times and is now on medication for mental illness. I engaged in other forms of occult practices not mentioned here. The author emphasizes that any form of the occult eventually leads to a life filled with misery, pain, and suffering and should be avoided at all costs.

2
Coming to Jesus

I gave my life to Jesus Christ in December 2019, and I was baptized. I had spent over twenty years of my life living a lie, believing it was the truth. I am not saying that I do not have my struggles, but living for Jesus is the best thing I could have ever done. I know that during my trials in life, I will get through them with God on my side. I appreciate that I can go to my Daddy [God] with my hopes, fears, troubles, and joys, and He will always be there for me.

Even in the church where I was baptized, they did not want me to attend due to some members, I believe, were afraid of what I had done. This was after I had to give my testimony before I was baptized. I learned that a church is only a building if they are not truly following Jesus. After I accepted Jesus into my life, I do not feel lonely anymore, knowing I have a relationship with God. People will let you down, but God won't ever leave you or forsake you. [Deuteronomy 31:8] "The Lord himself goes before you;

he will never leave you nor forsake you. Do not be afraid; do not be discouraged."

God loves us so much that it says He knows the number of hairs on our heads. [Matthew 10:26-31, NIV] "Are not two sparrows sold for a penny? Yet not one of them will fall to the ground outside your Father's care. And even the hairs of your head are all numbered. So, don't be afraid; you are worth more than many sparrows." Jeremiah 11 states, "Before I formed you in the womb, I knew you." God wants to have a relationship with us. Going to church all the time will not save you. You need to have a relationship with God, as stated in John 14:6, "Jesus said to him, 'I am the way, the truth, and the life. No one comes to the Father except through me.'"

We need to humble ourselves, come to Him, confess our sins, and repent. God knows that we are going to mess up, but when we do, we can go to Him, and He will forgive us. 1 John 1:9 states, "If we confess our sins, he is faithful and just to forgive us and to cleanse us from all unrighteousness." Luke 24:46-48 states, "…and repentance for the forgiveness of sins will be preached in his name to all nations, beginning in Jerusalem." Acts 3:18-19 states, "Repent, then, and turn to God, so that your sins may be wiped out, that times of refreshing may come from the Lord."

Jeremiah 31:34 says, "I will forgive their wickedness and will remember their sins no more. God doesn't just forgive. He chooses not to remember." There are many more verses in the Bible about sin and the need to repent. So, don't let that punk, the devil, try to condemn you and tell you that God did not forgive you and will hold your sins against you. This is a lie, for it states in the Word of God that He is faithful and just to forgive them and remember them no more.

Psalms 103:12 states, "He has removed our sins as far as the east is from the west." Another translation of this verse states, "…and as far as sunrise is from the sunset, he has separated us from our sins." Another translation states, "…as far as the east is from the west, so far has he removed our transgressions from us." Many times, including myself, we think God remembers our sins and will not forgive us because we messed up again. For this to be true, then God is a liar, but God can't lie, for it is not in His nature to lie.

It does not matter what sin we have done; Jesus paid the price by shedding His blood on the cross. He took on all the sins onto Himself as a penalty for our sins. 1 Peter 2:24 states, "…and He Himself bore our sins in His body on the cross so that we might die to sin and live to righteousness; for by His wounds, we are healed." In the Book of Romans (5: 8), it states, "But God demonstrates His own love for us in this: While we were still sinners, Christ died for us."

Jesus loved us so much that He was willing to be whipped, tortured, and killed in such a violent way for people who despised Him. He did this remarkable thing so that we can come to God and have a relationship with

Him. I know for myself I would not go to my death and go through all that had occurred for people who despise me. I do not believe most people would have gone through this, but Jesus loves us so much that He chose to come from Heaven, live among us, and go to His death for us.

If it were not for what He had done, I would go to Hell for my punishment for my sins, and I would deserve it. That is true love, for only a perfect sacrifice would cover our sins completely. In ancient times, they had to sacrifice animals to cover their sins, but this was a temporary covering of sins. When Jesus died on the cross, it was a perfect blood sacrifice. We are no longer required to have a blood sacrifice to wash our sins. Jesus, by dying on the cross, gave us a wonderful gift that no one else could have given.

God loves us so much that even for those who choose not to follow Him, He will not force them. I came to Jesus, and He accepted me as I was. God does not want us to stay as we were when we came to Him; He wants us to grow in our walk with Him. Even as I write this, I am still learning and growing, and this is what every Christian should hope for. Every day, we should grow in our walk with Him. We also need to let God remove things from our lives that He determines are not for our benefit. Just as we prune plants and remove weeds, we need to allow God to do this to us. We do this to help the plant grow better, and this is the same reason that God does this in our lives.

3
Warning to Parents

Parents need to spend time with their children and teach them the Word of God; this is what you are required to do. If you don't, they might seek out groups that are not beneficial to their well-being. This is the reason why some people might turn to groups like the occult, gangs, or other destructive associations, leading to their potential destruction. In such groups, they may engage in behaviors that are harmful to them, as they often seek love and acceptance outside their homes.

It's important to note that not all children will go down these paths, but the risk is there. Lives get busy, but as a parent, you have been given the gift and responsibility to raise your children. Unfortunately, many fathers abandon their children, leaving the mothers to raise them on their own. This often results in mothers working long hours to support their children, leading the kids to feel abandoned. It's only when they are older that they may realize their mothers were doing all they could to support them. Such behavior has been ongoing for too long and is unacceptable. Society would be better if we followed the family structure as God intended.

The breakdown of the family structure is often a contributing factor to the existence of many destructive groups. Teenage pregnancies, for example, can be linked to the absence of a father figure in a girl's life. Personally, I believe that if my father had been around, I might not have gotten involved in the groups that I did.

There are many things in society deemed normal that can open doors for the devil to have legal rights over individuals. Some of these things include reading horoscopes, using crystals from a Pagan Store, engaging in activities like Dungeons and Dragons, Pokémon, Tarot card reading, Ouija board, and watching movies based on the occult. Various video games with occult themes, such as Cultist Simulator, Dark Occultist, Dark Side Detective, Occult Chambers, Ghost Exile, Occultism: Interrogation, Call of Cthulhu, Occultist Night Cascades, and Occult, should be avoided. A new social media challenge called the Charlie Charlie challenge, where people summon a demon to ask it questions, is also something that should not be engaged in.

In the Bible, 1 Thessalonians chapter 5, verses 22 and 23 advise to abstain from all appearances of evil, seeking sanctification through God. It's crucial to be aware of the dangers associated with various games and challenges, especially those involving the summoning of demons. There are many good family games available that can be enjoyable without bringing destruction into your life. Christians need to be vigilant and aware of potentially harmful influences and avoid engaging in activities that may have negative spiritual consequences.

Galatians chapter 6 verse 7 warns not to be deceived, as God will not be mocked, and Exodus chapter 22 verse 18 states, "Thou shall not suffer a witch to live." Proverbs chapter 6, verses 16 to 19, list seven things that are abominations to God, including haughty eyes, a lying tongue, hands that shed innocent blood, a heart that devises wicked themes, feet that are swift to run into mischief, a false witness who utters lies, and one who sows discord among brothers. Leviticus chapter 20 verse 27 emphasizes the seriousness of certain practices, indicating that those involved should be put to death.

It is important to pray for individuals being deceived by the enemy and avoid actions that grieve the Holy Spirit. There are Christian games available that can help individuals learn about God, build their faith, and lead them towards Jesus. Parents should be aware of their children's activities and remember that they are parents, not just friends. It is their responsibility to look out for the welfare of their children. Engaging in dangerous activities out of curiosity can lead to serious consequences, and it's crucial for young people to resist peer pressure and strive to be leaders rather than followers.

These are just a few examples of things that can open doors to negative influences, and there are many more out there. Many movies are extremely violent and sexual, incorporating occult practices that can impact viewers spiritually. As Christians, it's essential to be discerning and avoid exposing ourselves to harmful content. Society often distorts what is good and evil, making it crucial for individuals to make decisions aligned with God's principles.

We watch these movies and call it entertainment, but it does affect us spiritually. Many of the children who watch these movies about magic want to be like the characters in the movie. When I was younger, I wanted to have the power they had in the movie. When you go to people who do palm reading, Tarot card reading, or any other forms of divination, these individuals cannot tell you the future. They tell you about the past and present because there is a familiar spirit (demon) that is telling them things. The demon does not know the future, and when you leave, the person sends the demon with you, making these things come true. Also, when these people contact your dead relative, it is not your loved one; it is a demon pretending to be your loved one who passed on. When someone dies, they either go to Hell or Heaven, depending on whether they had come to Jesus or not. In the Bible, Revelation 21 verse 8 warns about the fate of various sinful behaviors, including sorcery.

Scripture in Leviticus 19 verse 31 (ESV) emphasizes not turning to mediums or necromancers, stating that doing so will result in facing God's opposition and

Warning to Parents

being cut off from among the people. Exodus 22 verse 18 commands not permitting a sorcerer to live. Many other scriptures express God's disapproval of engaging in such practices. There are other things to avoid, such as paranormal activities involving ghosts, which are not spirits of deceased people but demons pretending to be the departed. Other practices like yoga, yin and yang, and recantation in Eastern philosophy can open doorways to negative influences, even though many churches are incorporating yoga.

Various games out there are considered very demonic. There is a YouTube video available for those interested, discussing these dangerous games. Some games, like "light as a feather and stiff as a board," popularized in the movie "The Craft," or the game "Bloody Mary," often played by teenagers, may seem fun but can lead to many problems. In my opinion, many Disney movies should be avoided as they have to do with the occult or are associated with homosexuality. A lot of secular music is very negative, with lyrics that are not uplifting and are detrimental to our spirituality. For example, the song from Metallica, "Fade to Black," talks about suicide as the only way out. Many people are suicidal, and when I felt depressed, I used to listen to this song and think about suicide. I know I was not alone in thinking about suicide as the only way out.

Here is another example from the band ACDC, which talks about going to Hell as the promised land. These songs, along with many others, open doors that should be closed spiritually. Some lyrics are offensive, but not everything you hear; it's what you don't hear that your subconscious picks up on. Much of the lyrics out there are bad enough. Some music uses profanity, sexual, and violent content. Is this the type of music you really want to be listening to? It is important to put good things into your body and not junk. Many people try to use excuses, saying that it is only entertainment. Another excuse they use is that they are just exercising their freedom of speech. My question is, if it is only entertainment, why does it affect the body and the way you think negatively? It makes sense that the devil would use music to deceive people since he was in charge of music in Heaven.

When it comes to secular music, if you insist on listening to it, make sure you ask the Holy Spirit to guide you. I don't recommend listening to the music out there, but I cannot stop you. Many bands will tell you that the occult and Satanism sell records. In Heaven, Lucifer was in charge of worship music, and even after being kicked out of Heaven, he still plays a part in the music in this world. I am not telling people what to do; they have to make their own decisions, but there are consequences for our actions, and are you willing to pay the penalty for these things? The Bible states that God will not be mocked and that what a man sows, he will reap. As for me and my house, we will serve the Lord. I should hate the things that he hates and love the things that he loves. If you listen to the Holy Spirit, he will always guide you down the correct path. In society, the goal is to make what is good into evil and what is evil into what is good. Also, to make a lie be the truth and the truth into a lie.

4
WHAT WE AS CHRISTIANS NEED TO DO

This is why we need to pray for our politicians, that they will act righteously before God. We should also pray for our teachers, asking that they impart truth to our children and avoid teaching them falsehoods. Intercession for pastors and the elders is crucial; we need them to teach the Word of God obediently to the congregation. As a church, we must build each other up rather than tear each other down.

It's disheartening to witness Christians who only portray their faith on Sundays and live as the world does the rest of the time. In these end days, we need to take our commitment to follow Jesus seriously. Unfortunately, some Christians treat church as a social gathering, and those who don't fit into their social group often feel unwelcome. In my early twenties, such exclusion impacted my perception of God, leading me to different forms of Paganism. It's vital for all Christians to sincerely search and pray to be the light of the world. If people don't see Jesus when they look at us, we need to reassess our focus.

Remaining focused on Jesus and obeying His commands is the right path. We don't know when Jesus will return for His church, so despite making mistakes, we must rise when knocked down and finish the race. After becoming a Christian, many old friends forgot about me, emphasizing lessons Christians can learn from the pagan community—particularly being more focused on worship and the sermon.

Many Christians could benefit from the pagan community's dedication during services, as some church members seem more interested in social media than the service itself. It appears that claiming church membership is considered more important than actually following Jesus. As Christians, we possess the truth, yet we often treat Jesus as an inconvenience. This raises the question: what is wrong with this picture? Jesus sacrificed everything for us, yet we become too busy to give Him anything.

Imagine neglecting to spend time with a spouse—what kind of relationship would that be? Likewise, we need to spend time in prayer and in the Word of God. In the Bible, Matthew 7:23 in the Amplified Bible warns that playing church without genuinely following Jesus risks hearing, "Depart from me, you workers of lawlessness." This is more frightening than the prospect of going to Hell, realizing we missed the mark despite thinking we did everything right. We cannot fool God; He sees us inside and out.

When we face our final moments, the ultimate desire is to hear God say, "Well done, good and faithful servant." In our prayers, it's crucial to avoid one-sided conversations where we do all the talking and neglect to allow God to speak to us. Prayer is meant to be a two-way communication, and our failure to listen shows selfishness. Often, we are quick to ask for everything but hesitant to let God request something from us. God desires a relationship with us, communicating His will, and we need to be attentive to what He wants to convey.

Acknowledging my own guilt in this regard, I apologize when I recognize this selfishness. Initiating the writing of this book was an act of obedience to God, even though it wasn't something I initially wanted to do. Fear gripped me, unsure of whether anyone would want to read it and what opinions they might form about me. At times, God may call us to uncomfortable tasks, emphasizing the importance of obedience to His will rather than our own desires.

Despite uncertainty about God's plans for me, I believe they will be amazing if I remain obedient. Our stories as Christians are not concluded but are just beginning. Despite feeling a calling to witness to more people after giving my life to Jesus, I struggle due to nervousness about my limited Bible knowledge and difficulties in communicating with strangers due to learning and other disabilities.

Nevertheless, I know I should step out in faith and share the message of Jesus with others.

Referencing Philippians 4:6-7, the Bible encourages believers not to be anxious but to present their requests to God through prayer and supplication. This passage assures that God's peace, surpassing understanding, will guard our hearts and minds through Christ Jesus. Despite fears, Jesus doesn't give us a spirit of fear but of sound mind. This implies that, with Jesus on our side, we can overcome our fears. Whenever we face fears, doubts, or obstacles hindering our Christian walk, we can boldly approach God's throne for help.

Access to God, once limited in the Old Testament, was granted through Jesus' sacrifice on the cross. Regardless of varying levels of knowledge about the Word of God, Christians, whether newly converted or seasoned, are all God's children. He wants us to come to Him with our hopes, fears, and concerns, desiring a relationship. Fear or any other obstacle should not hinder us from doing what God wants, a message directed not only to readers but also to myself.

Acknowledging fears, doubts, and hindrances is crucial, and relying on Jesus, we become more than conquerors. The Bible verse in Matthew 17:20-21 emphasizes that faith, even as small as a mustard seed, can move mountains. Trials and mountains in our lives may differ, but trusting in what Jesus said is paramount. Fear does not come from God but from the devil, who uses fear and guilt as weapons against Christians, aiming to hinder them from reaching their full potential in their walk with God.

The devil's goal is to divert our focus from Jesus. As followers of Jesus, our task is to keep our eyes on Him and advance God's kingdom. Life is not meant to be easy, but as we face challenges, we aim to hear God say, "Well done, good and faithful servant." Writing this book is a personal victory over the mountains and challenges set by the devil. Despite initial apprehension, the process brought a sense of accomplishment, aiming to reclaim what the devil had stolen.

The hope and prayer extend to all Christians, encouraging them to live obediently and fulfill what God wants them to be. The Apostle Paul's words in 2 Timothy 4:7, "I have fought the good fight; I have kept the faith," resonate as a reminder that life is temporary and a better place awaits believers. The prayer for all Christians is to hear God say, "Well done, good and faithful servant."

Acknowledging the persecution faced by Christians in different parts of the world, their focus remains on the prize of Heaven. Encouraging those who may not be obedient to God, the plea is to make the decision to change and follow Jesus. Christians are not alone on this journey; they have fellow believers to turn to for help and encouragement. Seeking help is not a sign of weakness, and admitting the need for assistance is crucial in dealing with life's challenges.

Regardless of the duration of one's Christian journey, God can use anyone who is willing. Having a humble heart and a willingness to be used by God is essential. No matter how much knowledge one possesses, God sees the real self, and honesty is paramount. Pride can hinder obedience, and Christians need to allow God to be God, remembering that it is His kingdom, not theirs.

The peace sign, often misunderstood, is explained as a broken upside-down cross with a circle around it, known as the cross of Nero. This symbolizes the destruction of Christians, serving as an example of how the world's perspective may differ from God's. To live obediently, Christians need to remain humble, avoid letting ego interfere, and focus on furthering God's kingdom.

There are places in various parts of the world where Christians face persecution, yet they remain focused on the ultimate prize—Heaven. If you find yourself not being obedient to God, make the decision to change and follow our King. It's crucial to remember that we are not alone on this journey; we have brothers and sisters in Christ to turn to for help and encouragement. From time to time, we all need assistance with the challenges life throws our way. There is nothing wrong or weak in admitting that we need help in dealing with issues.

This realization was difficult for me to accept, as I was accustomed to handling everything on my own. Regardless of how long you have been a Christian, God can use you as long as you are willing to be used by Him.

What We as Christians Need to Do

My hope and prayer for all Christians is to live and be obedient to God and what He wants us to do. What God might want you to do could take you out of your comfort zone, and that's okay. You might be scared about how you will get through it, but if God instructs you to do it, He will provide a way for you to accomplish it.

Uncertain about what God has in store for you, it's crucial to finish the race and upon reaching Heaven hear God say, "Well done, good and faithful servant." If you find yourself not being obedient to God, make the decision to change and be obedient. One way I am personally being obedient to God is by writing this book. Despite never envisioning myself as an author, I am both scared and excited about this endeavor. The excitement stems from doing what God wants, and the fear arises from feeling vulnerable as people learn about my life. This vulnerability led me to choose a pen name instead of using my real name.

For any Christian to be used by God, having a humble heart and a willingness to be used are essential. It doesn't matter if you just became a Christian or have been one for many years; God sees the real you. While you may fool people, you cannot fool God. If you have issues hindering your obedience to God, take them to Him and let Him bring about the necessary changes. It is God's kingdom, not ours, so we need to let God be God. Often, our ego (pride) gets in the way of doing what God wants.

Regardless of societal norms, what may seem foolish to the world is significant to God.

For instance, the so-called peace sign, often misunderstood, is explained as a broken upside-down cross with a circle around it, known as the cross of Nero. This symbolizes the destruction of Christians. It's disheartening to see many Christians wearing this symbol without understanding its true meaning. Attempting to enlighten them about the symbol's significance is met with varied responses—some listen, while others dismiss it, adhering to societal interpretations.

Wearing a symbol without researching its true meaning is foolish, and it reflects a lack of discernment. If it hurts to see Christians wearing such symbols, it likely hurts God's heart even more. On this journey, we are not alone; we have fellow believers whom we can and should turn to when we need help. Struggles are inevitable, and while we take those issues to God, He may also place people in our lives to assist us on this journey. Recognizing and appreciating these individuals is a blessing and a gift from God.

In modern society, there are numerous movies with occult themes that make witchcraft and the occult appear entertaining, even for children. Many of these movies are marketed as family-friendly, contributing to the exposure of young and impressionable minds to such content. Additionally, there are adult-oriented cartoons, like "Little Demon," depicting Satan as a father, which, though intended for adults, may attract children. These cartoons

What We as Christians Need to Do

often contain inappropriate content unsuitable for young audiences. Recently, I observed that there are plans to release Dungeon and Dragons (D&D) stamps, which, in my opinion, should be a source of concern for Christians. If it doesn't evoke anger, I wonder why not.

These forms of entertainment may seem harmless to some, but it's essential to see the bigger picture. There are plenty of good, family-friendly movies available that do not involve dark and potentially harmful themes. As Christians, it is crucial to stand up for what is right. While my opinion may not change many people's perspectives, if it helps even one person, I consider it a victory. There are numerous movies, songs, and other forms of media that subtly promote occult elements. If in doubt, seeking guidance from the Holy Spirit is essential. There are resources, including YouTube channels and other platforms, that expose the darkness present in various forms of media. Researching and understanding these issues can help Christians make informed choices about their entertainment.

It is worth noting that I have only scratched the surface of occult-related themes, and delving into all aspects would require an extensive discussion. My intention is not to encourage intrigue but to inform Christians about the potential dangers and how to avoid the traps set by the enemy. Drawing from my personal experience, I've been involved in certain pagan groups, and many others exist. While they may seem harmless initially, over time, one can realize their harmful nature and lack of truth. The ultimate truth lies in Jesus' words, as highlighted in the Bible, particularly in John 14:6, where Jesus says, "I am the way and the truth and the life. No one comes to the Father except through me." All other occult groups may claim to possess the truth, but they are mere counterfeits.

To draw a parallel, Secret Service agents spend considerable time examining real money, making it easy for them to recognize counterfeit bills. Similarly, spending time immersed in God's Word allows Christians to discern counterfeit teachings. However, some Christians may not recognize these counterfeits due to a lack of time spent in the Word. It is crucial to avoid deception and spend time understanding the Bible. I express concern about Christians who may unknowingly believe in counterfeits and stress the importance of spending time with God.

Acknowledging that the Bible might be perceived as challenging to read and comprehend, it's worth mentioning that numerous Bible versions are available. Additionally, for those who struggle with reading, audio versions of the Bible and various resources exist to aid in understanding. In the United States, where access to the Bible is relatively easy, it is important not to take this privilege for granted. Life may present challenges, but with God on our side, we are more than conquerors.

Whatever Christians do for God, even when unnoticed by others, matters because God sees it. Thus, it is essential to approach every task with a joyful heart and humility. Seeking approval from others is unnecessary as long as one knows in their heart that they are doing everything for Jesus. Christians are ambassadors for God in their communities, and their actions should point others to Jesus. Remaining focused on God's glory and maintaining a humble heart is crucial. God looks at the heart, not external appearances, and being genuine is more important than impressing people.

It is essential for Christians to recognize that God does not favor certain individuals over others, as expressed in Acts 10:34, where Peter says, "Truly I understand that God shows no partiality." To be a person that God can use, humility and a willingness to be used by God are vital. God does not appreciate pride but values those with humble hearts who desire to serve Him. People may fool others, but they cannot deceive God.

This section reminded me of the stories of Gideon and David from the Bible. Both individuals did not see themselves as worthy but desired to be used by God. Gideon's faithfulness led to a remarkable victory, and David, as a teenager, defeated Goliath through faith in God. These stories emphasize that anyone, regardless of perceived inadequacies, can be used by God if they are willing. Numerous stories throughout the Bible illustrate how individuals, despite their flaws, were used mightily by God. These individuals did not possess any extraordinary qualities but were willing to be instruments in God's hands.

In conclusion, being a person that God can use involves obedience, humility, and a desire to serve. Whether engaged in seemingly small or significant tasks, doing everything for God's glory is crucial. Even if the role appears thankless or less glamorous by societal standards, being obedient to God is the primary focus. Stories from the Bible, along with personal experiences, emphasize that anyone willing to be used by God can contribute significantly to His kingdom. The importance lies in obedience to our Savior, and the impact of our actions is ultimately determined by God, not by human approval or recognition.

When Jesus died on the cross, He paid the price for sin; the one who knew no sin became sin to be a perfect sacrifice, settling a debt we could never repay. Now, as children of the Highest King, we can boldly approach the throne of God. As Christians, it is imperative to be aware of the weapons and schemes of the enemy. We should exemplify the love of Jesus and pray for those being deceived. Many individuals have come out of the occult to embrace Christianity, serving our Lord and Savior, Jesus Christ.

It is crucial for us, as Christians, to refrain from casting aside these individuals. We must remember that the church belongs to Christ, not us, and we should not hinder what God wants to accomplish. When people come to Jesus, regardless of their background, it is essential to embrace them just as Jesus accepts them. In 2 Corinthians 5:17, it is stated, "Therefore, if anyone is in Christ, he is a new creation. The old has passed away; behold, the new has come." Recognizing them as new creations in Christ, we need to accept and welcome them, trusting that God has a plan for their lives.

As the Church of Jesus Christ, we must ask ourselves if we are truly doing what Jesus wants or merely playing church. Our lives should reflect Jesus, leading people to God rather than driving them away. It is inevitable that there will be people coming to Jesus whom we might question, but God will use anyone according to His plan. A biblical example is Saul, who persecuted Christians but transformed into a mighty man of God after encountering Jesus. His name changed to Paul, and he played a significant role in spreading the Gospel. This serves as a reminder that God can use individuals, even those with a challenging past.

Romans 3:23 reminds us that all have sinned and fallen short of the glory of God. The key takeaway is that if we align ourselves with the will of God and maintain a personal relationship with Jesus as our Lord and Savior, we will be with Him in Heaven. Deception is a real threat, emphasizing the need for consistent prayer and immersion in the Word of God to stay focused on His kingdom. While this book could delve into more details, trusting the Holy Spirit to guide decisions will lead to the right choices.

The author's prayer is that everyone makes the right decisions to serve God and fulfill His will. God has made His will evident through His Word, and daily engagement with Scripture is crucial for understanding Him. Building a relationship with God through communication is fundamental, as He desires an ongoing connection with us. Though challenging to write, the hope is that this book is both enjoyable and enlightening for those who read it.

Milton Keynes UK
Ingram Content Group UK Ltd.
UKHW020101050824
446426UK00013B/250